REVOLUTIONARY DISCOVERIES OF SCIENTIFIC PIONEERS™

JOHANNES KEPLER
AND THE
THREE LAWS
OF
PLANETARY MOTION

FRED BORTZ

ROSEN
PUBLISHING®

New York

Published in 2014 by The Rosen Publishing Group, Inc.
29 East 21st Street, New York, NY 10010

First Edition

Library of Congress Cataloging-in-Publication Data

Bortz, Fred, 1944–
Johannes Kepler and the three laws of planetary motion/Fred Bortz.
    pages cm.—(Revolutionary discoveries of scientific pioneers)
Includes glossary.
Includes bibliographical references and index.
ISBN 978-1-4777-1805-6 (library binding)
1. Kepler, Johannes, 1571–1630. 2. Astronomers—Germany—Biography.
3. Kepler's laws. 4. Planetary theory. I. Title.
QB36.K4B639 2014
521'.3—dc23

2013011700

Manufactured in the United States of America

CPSIA Compliance Information: Batch #W14YA: For further information, contact Rosen Publishing, New York, New York, at 1-800-237-9932.

A portion of the material in this book has been derived from *Kepler and the Laws of Planetary Motion* by Heather Hasan.

CONTENTS

4 INTRODUCTION

7 CHAPTER ONE:
SIGNS OF BRILLIANCE

20 CHAPTER TWO:
TURBULENT TIMES

32 CHAPTER THREE:
EARTH'S PLACE IN THE UNIVERSE

38 CHAPTER FOUR:
RIVALRY AND TRIUMPH

48 CHAPTER FIVE:
THE MATHEMATICS OF KEPLER'S LAWS

58 CHAPTER SIX:
KEPLER'S OTHER ACCOMPLISHMENTS AND
MODERN SCIENCE

66 TIMELINE
68 GLOSSARY
71 FOR MORE
INFORMATION
74 FOR FURTHER
READING
75 BIBLIOGRAPHY
77 INDEX

INTRODUCTION

As long as there have been civilizations on Earth, people have watched the skies with wonder. And wonder led to profound questions: What are those lights, both great and small? What makes them move the way they do? When and how did they come into being? Are they part of our world or separate from it?

Before there was science, ancient civilizations answered those questions with religion, stories, and myths. The sun became the greatest of all gods and ruled the day. The moon was a lesser god and ruled the night along with the stars.

Each civilization noticed that all the stars except five wanderers (which we now call the planets Mercury, Venus, Mars, Jupiter, and Saturn) moved together in patterns that we call constellations. The motions of the sun, the moon, and the planets took them across a set of constellations that formed a circle around the sky. We now call those constellations the zodiac.

The ancients noticed that the moon went through its phases in about twenty-nine days, during which it also moved through the zodiac. The sun's movement through that circle took much longer—about 365 days, and the seasons cycled once during that time.

The planets' motion was more complex. Each moved at its own speed and sometimes reversed direction and performed a loop before resuming its usual east-to-west

ÆTATIS
IG

JOHANNES KEPLER, SHOWN HERE IN THIS 1610 OIL PORTRAIT, LAID THE FOUNDATION FOR MODERN PLANETARY ASTRONOMY. HIS PRECISE OBSERVATIONS AND ANALYSIS LED TO THREE MATHEMATICAL LAWS THAT PRECISELY DESCRIBED THE ORBITS OF THE PLANETS, INCLUDING EARTH.

path. The planets, too, were usually considered gods, as were the constellations.

Because of modern science, we can now explain all those heavenly motions. We know that gravity holds the planets in orbit around the sun. We know that the sun is a star and that Earth is a planet in orbit around that star.

We can compute where the planets were in the sky at any time in history and where they will be at any time in the future. We can do the same for any other body in the solar system and any body in orbit around Earth or any other planet.

We can make those computations using a set of mathematical laws first recognized by a great astronomer and revolutionary thinker named Johannes Kepler.

SIGNS OF BRILLIANCE

W hen Johannes Kepler was born in the small town of Weil der Stadt, in Württemburg (now part of Germany), on December 27, 1571, the world, and especially Europe, was experiencing a period of great intellectual and social change. Protestant churches were challenging the religious and political dominance of the Roman Catholic Church. In science, leading astronomers were challenging Earth's central position in the universe.

No one could have predicted that Johannes, the firstborn child of Heinrich and Katharina Kepler, would grow up to be an astronomer, let alone challenge another idea central to both religious and scientific thinking: that the motion of each planet could be described by an interlocking set of perfect circles that turned at constant speeds.

He would replace each planet's set of circles with a single curved path and would develop mathematical formulas that related the sizes of those paths and speeds of all the planets in precise and simple ways. That curve and those formulas have been known ever since as Kepler's laws of planetary motion.

KEPLER'S EARLY YEARS

Johannes had a challenging childhood. His family had once been part of the nobility. However, their property, wealth, and status had dwindled over the generations, leaving the family poor. To earn a living for his family, Heinrich Kepler left them on several occasions to become a mercenary, or a paid soldier, for various religious causes. He left home when Johannes was five and only returned briefly and infrequently. Heinrich left the family for the last time when Kepler was in his late teens and is said to have died somewhere in the Netherlands.

Young Johannes lived with his mother, Katharina, at his grandfather's inn. Despite his young age, he was put to work there waiting tables. He often struggled with poor health. He suffered from stomach problems and often got rashes and boils on his skin. He was also nearsighted and had double vision, possibly caused by a near-fatal case of smallpox that he had suffered as a small child.

Despite those difficulties, he also had fond childhood memories that probably inspired him to become

KEPLER WAS BORN IN THE TOWN OF WEIL DE STADT, GERMANY, WHERE THIS MONUMENT NOW STANDS TO HONOR HIS PROMINENT ROLE IN THE HISTORY OF ASTRONOMY.

an astronomer. One of his earliest recollections was of a dark night in 1577 when his mother woke him and brought him to a nearby hillside to see a brilliant comet in the sky. On another clear night in 1580, his mother took him out to view a lunar eclipse. He watched the moon darken and then brighten as Earth's shadow passed across it.

Despite poverty and illness, Johannes was a gifted student. The Kepler family's move from Weil der Stadt to the nearby town of Leonberg gave young Johannes greater educational opportunity. At the German *Schreibschule* in Leonberg, his teachers recognized that he was much brighter than the rest of the boys. They sent him to a Latin school to prepare him for university. At the Latin school, Kepler's instructors taught him so well that, for the rest of his life, he spoke and wrote clearly and beautifully in Latin. His German, however, was clumsy and confused.

His education was interrupted for a year when his grandfather decided that the boy had received enough education and put him to work as a dishwasher. His teachers begged his grandfather to let him return to school. Thankfully, the grandfather agreed.

Johannes was a hardworking boy who had a great thirst for knowledge. However, he was also fiercely competitive. Nothing annoyed him more than the thought that one of his classmates had outdone him. Because of those traits, his classmates considered him

SCIENCE AND RELIGION IN THE RENAISSANCE

Kepler lived in a period of European history that we now call the Renaissance, which was marked by rapidly spreading knowledge and changing ideas. Thanks to the invention of the printing press in the fifteenth century, ancient texts, which previously spread slowly as hand-copied documents, became available to scholars everywhere as printed books.

The ancient manuscripts had survived a difficult period in European history known as the Middle Ages largely through the efforts of Arab and Persian scholars and Christian monks, who painstakingly hand-copied and translated their texts. Like the ancient philosophers, these scholars drew no distinction between the religious and scientific quest for knowledge. For that reason, young Johannes Kepler's interest in astronomy blended well with his religious studies.

Although those ancient texts were still considered important sources for astronomers, Kepler also studied newer works, including *De Revolutionibus Orbium Coelestium* ("On the Revolutions of the Heavenly Spheres") by Nicolaus Copernicus (1473–1543). *De Revolutionibus*, which was still considered controversial decades after its publication in 1543, described a universe centered on the sun (heliocentric), with Earth as one planet among others, rotating and traveling around it.

Not only did Kepler accept Copernicus's idea of a heliocentric universe, he also built on and refined it. It led to the laws of planetary motion that became his legacy. Thus in his later years, Kepler, like Copernicus, promoted ideas about planetary motion that conflicted with those of the leaders of his church, even while remaining loyal to it.

a know-it-all. Occasionally, that led to outbursts and fistfights. Later in life, he admitted that his classmates' anger toward him was often his own fault.

He also had a deep religious faith. In 1584, when he was just twelve, he enrolled in the Adelberg convent school to prepare for a career as a Lutheran clergyman. He was given free room and board, which allowed him to finally escape his distracting household. Then, in 1589, he enrolled at the University of Tübingen.

CHANGES OF DIRECTION

When Kepler entered the University of Tübingen, he planned to become a Lutheran priest. With that goal in mind, he took courses in philosophy and theology (the study of religion). However, he excelled in mathematics, which, at that time, included astronomy. The late sixteenth century was an exciting time to study astronomy, and Kepler was fortunate to study with one of the most respected astronomy teachers in Europe, Michael Maestlin (1550–1631).

Maestlin had written a textbook that was based on an ancient book called the *Almagest* by Claudius Ptolemy, a Greek mathematician and astronomer who lived in the second century CE in Alexandria, Egypt. To understand the motion of the heavenly bodies, Ptolemy developed a geocentric (Earth-centered) description. The sun, moon, and planets followed paths around an unmoving Earth at the center of everything.

THIS 1754 PAINTING SHOWS THE EGYPTIAN-BORN GREEK MATHEMATICIAN AND ASTRONOMER CLAUDIUS PTOLEMY MEASURING THE POSITION OF AN OBJECT IN THE HEAVENS WITH A QUADRANT. BEHIND HIM IS THE GODDESS ASTRONOMIA. PTOLEMY'S GREAT BOOK, THE *ALMAGEST*, WRITTEN IN 150 CE, DESCRIBED THE MOTION OF THE SUN, MOON, PLANETS, AND STARS IN A HELIOCENTRIC OR EARTH-CENTERED UNIVERSE.

Ptolemy's description was based on the teachings of the fourth-century BCE Greek philosopher Aristotle (384–322 BCE) and the Greek mathematician Eudoxus (c. 408–347 BCE), who, in turn, drew on earlier ideas of heavenly perfection from their great teacher Plato. The paths of the sun, moon, and planets had to be

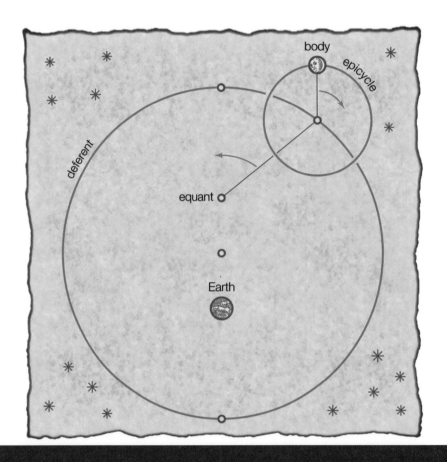

IN THE *ALMAGEST*, PTOLEMY DESCRIBED THE MOTION OF THE SUN, THE MOON, OR A PLANET AS A COMBINATION OF TWO CIRCULAR MOTIONS AT CONSTANT RATES. THE BODY'S MAIN MOTION WAS AROUND A LARGE CIRCLE CALLED THE DEFERENT, WHICH WAS CENTERED ON A POINT HALFWAY BETWEEN EARTH AND ANOTHER POINT CALLED THE EQUANT. FOR EACH BODY, A SMALLER CIRCLE CALLED THE EPICYCLE WAS CENTERED ON A POINT THAT TRAVELED AROUND THE DEFERENT. THE SUN'S SPEED AROUND THE DEFERENT WAS NOT CONSTANT. INSTEAD, ITS SPEED VARIED SO THAT THE ANGLE IT MADE WITH THE EQUANT CHANGED AT A CONSTANT RATE.

perfect. But to make those perfect motions fit with observations led to complications.

Plato knew that the planets appeared to speed up and slow down as they moved through the constellations of the zodiac, even occasionally reversing direction in a looping motion before resuming their usual east-to-west march. Plato was sure that a mathematical solution could bring this apparent contradiction into line with his description of the universe, and Eudoxus and Aristotle took important steps toward that solution.

Eudoxus envisioned sets of four spheres, one set for each of the five known planets (Mercury, Venus, Mars, Jupiter, and Saturn). Each planet sat on the equator of one of those four spheres, which was connected to the second sphere in the set. The second sphere was connected to a third, which was finally connected to a fourth. The fourth sphere for each planet was centered on Earth, and they all turned like the gears of a mechanical clock.

A large sphere, known as the vault of heaven, surrounded all of these. This final sphere contained the stars and rotated so that they also moved from east to west across the sky. This construction was bulky, but it allowed a geocentric universe to match the observed motions of the planets. The moon and the sun needed only three spheres each in Eudoxus's description. And the vault of heaven did not need any additional spheres. All these groups of spheres rotated around Earth, but none of them were linked to each other.

Aristotle extended Eudoxus's idea. He linked the motion of each set of spheres to the others. He believed the universe must fit together in a connected system. He looked for a linkage that explained the motion of each part of the system in relation to all the others. Thus, like gears working together in a machine, when the spheres of one planet turned, they had an effect on the motion of the other planets' spheres. To make that work, Aristotle had to add even more spheres, eventually coming up with a universe of fifty-five spheres.

Ptolemy's description of the universe had fewer spheres but retained two important principles of Aristotle's version. Motion of heavenly bodies had to be in perfect circles at constant speed, and Earth was at the center of everything. In the *Almagest*, he included three mathematical elements to bring the planets' motions in line with observation. Instead of having Earth at the exact center of the planets' circular paths, he added a point called the equant.

The sun traveled in a circle around Earth, but its speed on that circle was not constant. Instead, the angle it made with the equant changed at a constant rate. The midpoint of the line segment between Earth and the equant was the center of a circle called the deferent, or the main circular path, for each planet. The equant and deferent were still not enough to solve the mismatch between his math and the actual motion, so for each planet, he added a smaller circle, called an epicycle, going around a point on the larger circle. That seemed to solve the problem.

But over time, as astronomers gathered more measurements with better tools, Ptolemy's description needed to be modified. The solution was simple to devise, but it made the motion seem even more complex. They added epicycles to the epicycles.

Maestlin's textbook taught the ideas of Ptolemy, but outside his classroom, Maestlin privately told his students about Polish astronomer Nicolaus Copernicus, including his controversial *De Revolutionibus*. By moving the sun to the central position of the universe, Copernicus removed the need for the equant and deferent and reduced the number of epicycles.

Kepler immediately recognized the value of Copernicus's ideas. Despite his interest in theology, he became fascinated by Copernicus's new direction in astronomy, and that fascination ultimately changed the direction of his life as well.

A CAREER IN SCIENCE

As Kepler was finishing his education in Tübingen, he made an important decision that would change the direction of his life and the course of history. His teachers selected him to go to Graz, now part of Austria, where he would teach mathematics at a

small school. He had always wanted to be a priest, but Maestlin's urgings persuaded him to accept the teaching position. At the age of twenty-two, Kepler abandoned his dream of becoming a priest and began a career in the study of science.

In Graz, Kepler was free to explore all of the scientific ideas that had so excited him when he was at the

University of Tübingen. He asked questions about the universe that other people took for granted. He wanted to know what the world was made of. He also wanted to know why there were only six planets (at the time, only Mercury, Venus, Earth, Mars, Jupiter, and Saturn were known to exist). Further, Kepler wanted to know why the planets were situated where they were in the sky. He questioned what determined the distance between their orbits.

These questions ultimately led him to three laws that led on one hand to the triumph of Copernicus's heliocentric universe and on the other hand to the end of one of its central principles.

CHAPTER TWO

TURBULENT TIMES

Johannes Kepler lived most of his life in turbulent times for both religion and science. New ideas were swirling that challenged longtime religious and political authorities in Europe. Science was casting doubt on long-accepted ideas about the universe and Earth's place in it. As is often the case, the people who were proposing new ways of thinking faced powerful opposition from authorities who did not want to give up the old ways and ideas.

RELIGIOUS REFORMATION AND POLITICAL CONFLICT

When Kepler was born and for much of his life, Europe was in the midst of religious upheaval and conflict. For centuries, a Catholic emperor,

KEPLER LIVED IN A TIME OF DYNAMIC CHANGES IN SCIENCE AND RELIGION. IN 1517 MARTIN LUTHER BEGAN THE PROTESTANT REFORMATION BY CHALLENGING CERTAIN BELIEFS OF THE ROMAN CATHOLIC CHURCH. HE NAILED A DOCUMENT THAT HAS BECOME KNOWN AS HIS 95 THESES TO THE DOOR OF THE CHURCH IN WITTENBERG, GERMANY. OTHER PRIESTS AND CHURCH MEMBERS AGREED WITH HIM AND SPLIT OFF TO CREATE THEIR OWN FORM OF CHRISTIANITY. SOON MUCH OF EUROPE WAS ENGAGED IN RELIGIOUS WAR. WHEN KEPLER WAS BORN IN 1571, AN UNEASY PEACE PREVAILED. BUT WAR WOULD AGAIN BREAK OUT IN HIS LIFETIME.

who was given the title Holy Roman Emperor by the Pope, ruled most of Europe. People did not have religious freedom. They were required to follow the religion of their ruler, even if they did not believe in its teachings. But a period known as the Protestant Reformation began in 1517, well before Kepler was born, and led to religious and political upheavals that lasted for decades.

The Reformation started with a dramatic action by Martin Luther (1483–1546), a German monk and teacher. He posted a list of complaints against the Catholic Church on the door of a church in Wittenberg, Germany. Luther, and soon other reformers and their followers, believed that the Roman Catholic Church was corrupt and needed to be changed. They became known as Protestants.

The Protestants were particularly displeased with the fact that priests and monks frequently sold forgiveness to the people. Luther and others like him believed that sin was forgiven through faith in God's grace alone, not by anything that people could do, such as doing good deeds or giving money to the church.

Luther's protest spread rapidly and split Europe into two groups. Catholics and Protestants bitterly opposed each other. Years of violent religious conflict followed. Hostilities lasted until 1555, when the warring sides reached a compromise called the Peace of Augsburg. With this settlement, each prince was given the right to decide what religion (Catholicism or Protestantism) would be practiced within his state.

The peace was uneasy, and religious warfare broke out once again during Kepler's lifetime. The early seventeenth century saw the beginning of the Thirty Years' War (1618–1648), a German civil war, which soon involved nearly all of Europe. This war resulted in the devastation of large areas of central Europe and the death of one-third of its population. This religious unrest greatly affected Kepler's life and work.

FACING RELIGIOUS PERSECUTION

The city of Tübingen devoutly followed Luther's ideas. When Kepler moved to Graz to teach, however, he found a much more unstable religious atmosphere. In Graz, Catholics and Protestants lived side by side, and this led to religious conflict.

While Kepler was living in Graz, Archduke Ferdinand II assumed rule over inner Austria, which included Graz. While Ferdinand's father had tolerated Protestants in his lands, Ferdinand would not. Archduke Ferdinand sought to restore Catholic domination in Europe.

Under his rule began what was called the Counter-Reformation, a movement that fought to stop the spread of Protestantism. Life was made difficult for

the Protestants who were living in Graz. Eventually, the Lutheran school in which Kepler taught was closed, and he and the other Protestant teachers were forced from the city on threat of death.

Though Kepler was initially allowed to return to Graz, he was later kicked out for good when he refused to convert from Protestantism to Catholicism. It was this religious persecution that brought him into the company of Tycho Brahe (1546–1601), a well-known Danish astronomer of the time. Having been relieved of his teaching job in Graz, Kepler readily accepted Brahe's offer to join him in his work in Prague. The work that he did

AFTER COMPLETING HIS STUDIES IN TÜBINGEN, KEPLER MOVED TO GRAZ, AUSTRIA, TO TAKE A POSITION TEACHING MATHEMATICS IN A LUTHERAN SCHOOL. UNFORTUNATELY, THE CATHOLIC ARCHDUKE FERDINAND II, SHOWN HERE, SOON ASSUMED RULE OVER INNER AUSTRIA, WHICH INCLUDED GRAZ. HE CLOSED THE LUTHERAN SCHOOL AND EVENTUALLY FORCED KEPLER AND OTHER PROTESTANT TEACHERS TO LEAVE UNLESS THEY CONVERTED TO CATHOLICISM.

HOW RELIGIOUS PERSECUTION CHANGED SCIENCE

Throughout history, scientists have often been religious, even at times when their faith and their science led to different conclusions. While remaining loyal to their faiths, the Catholic Copernicus and Protestant Kepler were willing to challenge religious doctrine if it was in conflict with what they and others observed.

When religious authorities also held political power, such scientists often found themselves in trouble because of their scientific theories, research, and conclusions. But history also shows us that scientists have sometimes had difficulties with the authorities because of their religious background alone. Kepler, for example, lost his position at Graz because he would not convert to Catholicism. He found new work in Tycho Brahe's observatory, where his observations led to his famous three laws that changed the course of astronomy.

But history has been marked by much more severe episodes of religious persecution, and these, too, affected science in unexpected ways. Jews have historically faced prejudice (called anti-Semitism) wherever they lived. In the nineteenth and early twentieth centuries, many European Jews chose to convert to Christianity rather than face the obstacles that Jews had in getting into certain universities or professions. This was especially true of Jewish scientists who were not observant and wanted to fit in with their educated neighbors and colleagues.

When Adolf Hitler and the Nazi Party came to power in Germany in the 1930s, they began passing laws that kept Jews out of positions of responsibility. They defined a person as a Jew if that person had Jewish ancestry, even if he or she had converted or had married a non-Jew. As a result, many scientists with Jewish connections (including those who were Christian converts, children of converts, or had Jewish spouses) fled Germany and other European countries where the Nazis began to have influence. If they had remained, they would probably have been among the millions who lost their lives in Nazi death camps.

Ironically, many of those refugees came to the United States, where they played important roles in the development of the atomic bomb during World War II. The world would be very different today if Hitler's scientists had developed it first.

with Brahe would ultimately lead to his discovery of the laws of planetary motion.

AN ORDERLY UNIVERSE

Kepler was a very religious man. He converted to Protestantism at a very young age. Though he ultimately abandoned his dream of becoming a priest, his religious devotion greatly affected his work. He thought it was his religious duty to work toward understanding the universe that God had created. He made references to God throughout his writing. He was convinced that God had created the universe according to a mathematical plan.

This belief in an orderly universe traces back at least as far as Plato. It is the reason for the perfect circular motions that Aristotle described, and it led Ptolemy to add the deferent, equant, and epicycles to match the observed motions of the sun, the moon, and the planets. Kepler believed a universe that had been created by such an intelligent God would have to be one of perfect mathematical order. He felt that the mind of God was mathematical and that the more we thought in numbers, the clearer our thinking would be.

He became obsessed with finding God's harmony in nature. Perhaps it was the religious conflict of the time that led him to search the heavens for celestial harmony. He even thought that the planets made sounds as they moved, the way that the strings of a lyre do as they are played.

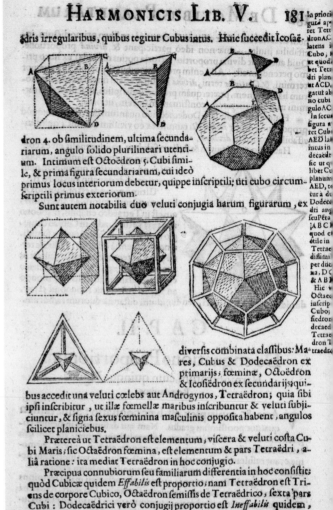

KEPLER CONSIDERED IT HIS RELIGIOUS DUTY TO FIND MATHEMATICAL HARMONY IN THE UNIVERSE. HE KNEW THAT THERE ARE ONLY FIVE POSSIBLE SOLID SHAPES THAT HAVE IDENTICAL REGULAR POLYGONS AS THEIR SIDES. FOR EXAMPLE, THE CUBE HAS SIX SIDES THAT ARE IDENTICAL SQUARES. THOSE SOLIDS CAN CONTAIN PERFECT SPHERES THAT TOUCH THEIR SIDES, AND THEY CAN BE WITHIN PERFECT SPHERES THAT TOUCH THEIR POINTS. ON PAGE 181 OF KEPLER'S 1619 BOOK *HARMONICE MUNDI (HARMONY OF THE WORLD)*, HE DESCRIBES AN ARRANGEMENT OF SPHERES AND SOLIDS SO THAT THE SIX PLANETS' ORBITS ARE ON SPHERES WITH THE FIVE DIFFERENT PERFECT SOLIDS BETWEEN THEM.

Kepler's book *Harmonice Mundi* (*Harmony of the World*; 1619) demonstrates these theories. It also contains the third of his three laws of planetary motion.

While Kepler searched for harmony, however, his life was anything but harmonious. The religious zeal of the sixteenth and seventeenth centuries led to witch-hunting hysteria. People were obsessed with identifying and executing people they suspected of being witches.

His mother was one of the many people charged with practicing witchcraft. Kepler came to his mother's defense, writing letters and petitioning the court to drop the charges. The trial went on for years before Katharina Kepler was finally released.

HEAVENLY INFLUENCES

Despite all of this trouble and the start of the Thirty Years' War, Kepler continued to work. While teaching in Graz, he was also district mathematician. In this position, he surveyed the land, settled disputes over the accuracy of weights and measures used in business, and made calendars.

Besides listing the days of the week and the dates of the months, calendars today usually include information about holidays, the phases of the moon (full, new, etc.), and the changes of seasons marked by the vernal and autumnal equinoxes at the beginning of spring and fall, and the solstices at the beginning of summer and winter.

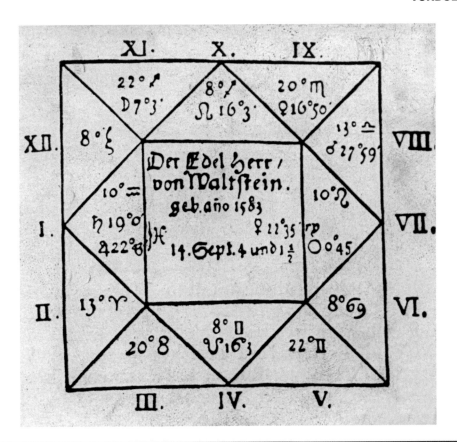

In Kepler's time, people also expected the calendar to make predictions for their everyday lives that were based on the positions of the heavenly bodies, including the stars and planets. Observing the stars and planets was then and is today part of the science called astronomy. Predicting their effect on human life, which we now call astrology, was also considered a science. On his calendars, Kepler gave advice to farmers about when they should plant and harvest their crops. He also gave advice to military and political leaders. He even offered advice on matters of romance.

Today, we know that the positions of the sun and moon, along with the tilt of Earth on its axis, determine such things as the tides, the seasons of the year, the phases of the moon, and the eclipses of the sun and moon. These occurrences can be important to the plans of farmers and military leaders. A farmer knows that there are certain times when it is better to plant and harvest crops. A military leader may wish to plan an attack to fit seasonal conditions or the amount of moonlight at night.

We also know that the positions of the planets and stars in the sky have no effect on conditions on Earth. Thus we no longer consider astrology a science. Kepler was one of the first to question its value. He knew that by studying which of his predictions were correct, he could test it. In 1601, he wrote a book titled *De Fundamentis Astrologiae Certioribus* (*Concerning the More Certain Fundamentals of Astrology*). In it, he concluded that believing that the stars determine what happens in people's lives was a superstition. Trusting astrological predictions could be risky!

COPERNICUS AND KEPLER, TWO REVOLUTIONARY THINKERS

Kepler's work not only upset the beliefs of people accustomed to following the predictions of astrology, it also challenged the Catholic and Protestant churches. Before Nicolaus Copernicus published *De Revolutionibus* in 1543, church doctrine placed Earth and humanity at the center of the universe. Despite the growing acceptance of a heliocentric universe among scholars, Catholic doctrine did not change for nearly three hundred years. It was not until 1822 that the Catholic Church permitted publication of heliocentric books in Rome.

Kepler accepted Copernicus's heliocentric idea, but he also found parts of *De Revolutionibus* troubling. The need for epicycles upon epicycles to explain the motion of the planets conflicted with his idea that heavenly motions should follow simple mathematical rules. It would take his work with Tycho Brahe and another burst of revolutionary thinking to replace those troublesome chains of circles with three harmonious laws of planetary motion. And that, in turn, made it easier for people to accept that Earth rotated on its axis daily and followed a yearly path around the sun.

CHAPTER THREE

EARTH'S PLACE IN THE UNIVERSE

Although Copernicus deserves credit for changing scientific thinking from a geocentric to a heliocentric universe, he was not the first person to write about it. The idea can be traced back almost two thousand years earlier to the Greek mathematician and philosopher Aristarchus of Samos (310–230 BCE). Although Aristarchus's heliocentric description of the universe was as fully developed as Aristotle's geocentric one, his ideas gained little support among philosophers and astronomical scholars. By the Middle Ages, Aristarchus's ideas were barely known and were largely ignored.

Like the Catholics in Copernicus's time, the leaders of Kepler's Protestant Church rejected the idea of a heliocentric universe. The Bible places humans at the center of God's attention, so the world must be the center of everything. Most people followed

THIS DIAGRAM SHOWS COPERNICUS'S HELIOCENTRIC UNIVERSE. IT REFLECTS THE STATE OF KNOWLEDGE IN THE EARLY SEVENTEENTH CENTURY. THE SUN IS AT THE CENTER WITH THE ORBITS OF THE PLANETS GOING OUTWARD: MERCURY, VENUS, EARTH AND THE MOON, MARS, JUPITER WITH ITS FOUR GALILEAN MOONS, AND SATURN. AROUND THE OUTSIDE ARE THE GERMAN NAMES OF THE TWELVE CONSTELLATIONS OF THE ZODIAC.

their religious leaders' viewpoint. Besides, the Copernican ideas go against common experience. If Earth rotates on its axis, why do objects fall straight down when dropped? And what keeps the things on the surface of Earth from flying off?

The Copernican model greatly appealed to Kepler, however. It fit both his scientific and religious sense. By eliminating the deferent, the equant, and some epicycles, it seemed more perfect mathematically. That fit his ideas of mathematics being the language of God. Furthermore, Kepler believed the sun was God's most brilliant heavenly creation. In fact, he believed the sun represented God. Therefore, he felt it was only fitting that the sun should be at the center of the universe, with Earth and the other planets revolving around it. He also believed the force that drove the planets to revolve around the sun came from the sun itself. This faith that Kepler had in the sun would play a big part in his later discoveries.

GALILEO AND KEPLER'S *MYSTERIUM*

The title of *Mysterium Cosmographicum* conveys a sense of Kepler's mystic side. In his quest to discover mathematical perfection in the universe, he would sometimes stretch beyond what the observations actually implied. According to Alan W. Hirschfeld in his book *Parallax: The Race to Measure the Cosmos*, Galileo's response did not discuss Kepler's geometric theory, which probably appeared as odd to Galileo as it does to modern scientists. Kepler may have misinterpreted Galileo's positive statement about Copernicus's theory as support for his own mathematical results.

Hirschfeld notes that Kepler wrote back with passion, "urging Galileo to go public in support of the Copernican system." However, "Galileo didn't share the enthusiasm of his German counterpart, whose verbal bravado marked him as a trigger-happy Copernican zealot (which he was)… Twelve years would pass before Galileo wrote to Kepler again."

HEAVENLY PERFECTION

While teaching a geometry class in Graz, Kepler had a revelation that he thought could lead him to the mathematical orderliness of the universe. He drew an equilateral triangle (a triangle with all three sides—and all three angles—equal to each other) within a circle. He then drew another circle within the triangle. It suddenly occurred to him that the ratio of the larger circle to the smaller circle was the same as the

MATHEMATICIANS HAVE KNOWN SINCE ANCIENT TIME THAT THESE FIVE REGULAR SOLID SHAPES ARE THE ONLY ONES POSSIBLE. THEIR FACES ARE IDENTICAL REGULAR POLYGONS THAT MEET AT IDENTICAL ANGLES. REGULAR POLYGONS HAVE STRAIGHT-LINE SIDES OF EQUAL LENGTHS WITH EQUAL ANGLES BETWEEN THE SIDES. FROM TOP LEFT, THE SHAPES ARE THE ICOSAHEDRON (20 SIDES), THE DODECAHEDRON (12 SIDES), THE HEXAHEDRON OR CUBE (6 SIDES), THE TETRAHEDRON (4 SIDES), AND THE OCTAHEDRON (8 SIDES). KEPLER TRIED TO DEVELOP AN ARRANGEMENT OF ORBITS OF THE SIX PLANETS SEPARATED BY THE FIVE REGULAR SOLIDS.

ratio of the orbits of Saturn and Jupiter. Kepler was very excited by his finding. Could geometric figures fit into the spaces between the orbits of all the planets? He began to look for patterns within the orbits of the planets using other shapes.

Eventually, he looked toward the five Platonic shapes, or "perfect solids," that had been used by the ancient Greeks. The faces of those solids are regular polygons that, like the equilateral triangle, have all their sides and angles equal. Geometric analysis shows that only five of these can exist: the four-sided tetrahedron with triangular sides, the six-sided hexahedron or cube with square sides, the eight-sided octahedron (triangles), the twelve-sided dodecahedron (pentagons), and the twenty-sided ico-sahedron (triangles). These three-dimensional shapes were able to fit exactly into a sphere so that all of their points touched the sphere.

To Kepler, the Platonic solids explained why there could only be six planets including Earth, which was the number of planets known to exist at the time. With six planets, there would be a total of five spaces between them, one space for each Platonic solid. He felt that the Platonic solids determined the distances between the planets. He planned to build a copper model of his geometrical design, but he only succeeded in building a paper one.

Kepler was excited by his geometric theory, and he immediately began working on a book to explain his ideas. It took him a year to write the book, which he titled *Mysterium Cosmographicum* (*Cosmographic Mystery*).

When the book was published in 1596, Kepler sent copies of it to Italian astronomer and mathematician Galileo Galilei (1564–1642) and Brahe. Galileo responded courteously and with thanks, stating that he, too, accepted Copernicus's heliocentric interpretation, though he was reluctant to declare it publicly. Brahe, however, was immediately intrigued. Even though he did not give up his belief in Ptolemy's geocentric universe, he recognized that Copernicus's heliocentric universe was useful for making calculations. He wrote a glowing letter to Kepler in support of *Mysterium Cosmographicum.* That letter would change the direction of Kepler's life.

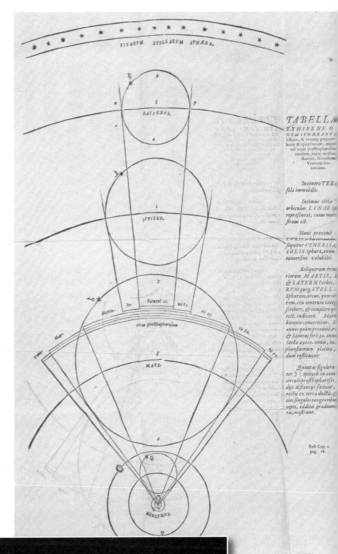

JOHANNES KEPLER PUBLISHED THIS ILLUSTRATION IN THE 1621 EDITION OF *MYSTERIUM COSMOGRAPHICUM (COSMOGRAPHIC MYSTERY)*. KEPLER HAD JUST DISCOVERED HIS THREE LAWS OF PLANETARY MOTION AS A RESULT OF CALCULATING THE ORBIT OF MARS FROM TYCHO BRAHE'S DATA. HE THEN APPLIED THE LAWS TO THE ORBITS OF THE OTHER PLANETS. THE ILLUSTRATION ALSO SHOWS THE ORBITS OF THE MOON AND THE FOUR MOONS OF JUPITER THAT GALILEO DISCOVERED. THE ORBITS OF THOSE FOUR MOONS FOLLOWED KEPLER'S LAWS JUST AS THE SIX KNOWN PLANETS DID IN THEIR PATHS AROUND THE SUN.

RIVALRY AND TRIUMPH

*T*ycho Brahe was one of the best astronomers of his time for two reasons. First, he had the finest equipment of any observatory of the time before the invention of the astronomical telescope. Because of that, he became well known for the accuracy with which he calculated the changing positions of the moon, Mars, and the other planets. Second, he kept excellent records over a long working lifetime.

The observatory and his data were enough to secure his place in history, but Brahe believed he was destined for even greater fame as the person who had finally understood the motion of the heavens. He combined what he thought were the best parts of Copernicus's heliocentric system with the geocentric universe of Ptolemy to produce a description he called the Tychonic system.

TYCHO BRAHE'S OBSERVATORY NEAR PRAGUE HAD THE FINEST EQUIPMENT OF ANY IN THE WORLD BEFORE THE INVENTION OF THE TELESCOPE. HE BECAME WELL KNOWN FOR HIS ACCURATE DATA ABOUT THE MOTION OF THE MOON AND THE PLANETS, ESPECIALLY MARS. KEPLER'S INVITATION TO JOIN BRAHE'S LABORATORY CHANGED HIS LIFE. AFTER BRAHE'S DEATH, KEPLER WAS ABLE TO CONTINUE TAKING MEASUREMENTS AND EVENTUALLY USED THE OBSERVATORY'S VAST COLLECTION OF DATA TO DEVELOP HIS THREE LAWS OF PLANETARY MOTION.

A HISTORIC INVITATION

The Tychonic system correctly put the planets into orbits around the sun and had the moon in orbit around Earth. However, like Ptolemy, Brahe thought the sun and the stars revolved around Earth. Still it was a challenge to understand how the heavenly motions all fit together. When he read Kepler's *Mysterium Cosmographicum*, Brahe called the work brilliant. Even though the book was based on a Copernican sun-centered universe, Brahe recognized Kepler's mathematical genius. The young astronomer could be very useful in analyzing Brahe's measurements to prove that the Tychonic system was correct.

Kepler was thrilled when he received Brahe's letter praising his work. He was also in need of employment since his school in Graz had closed. In 1600, Brahe invited Kepler to come to Prague, a town not far from Graz, to work with him, an invitation that would change history. He was eager to see Brahe's careful measurements of the changing positions of the moon, Mars, and the other planets, which Brahe had carefully collected over the previous twenty years. With that data, Kepler hoped to improve on Copernicus's model of the solar system.

Brahe had gathered that data in his observatory in Castle Benátky, near Prague. Among its outstanding instruments were quadrants, large devices that he used to determine the heights of stars and planets

TYCHO BRAHE LIVED IN THE CASTLE OF BENATEK NEAR PRAGUE (THE CAPITAL OF THE MODERN CZECH REPUBLIC) FROM AUGUST 1599 TO JUNE 1600. THAT WAS WHERE KEPLER FIRST MET HIM IN FEBRUARY 1600.

above the horizon. Brahe's observatory also had giant wood and metal sextants to measure the angle between two objects, such as planets or stars. He also had a great armillary sphere, which he used to obtain the positions of stars. Also in the observatory was a magnificent brass globe on which Brahe had engraved the results of his careful observations, the positions of a thousand stars.

MISMATCHED EXPECTATIONS

Kepler and Brahe had a rocky relationship. When Kepler agreed to go to Prague, he had thought he would be treated as an equal to Brahe and would have access to all Brahe's measurements. Instead, Brahe treated Kepler as an assistant and servant. He was also mistrustful and refused to share the data that Kepler had been so eager to see.

Finally, however, Brahe reluctantly gave Kepler an assignment to analyze some of that collected data. As Brahe grew older, he felt that he was racing against death and his life dream of establishing the Tychonic system as the correct conception of the universe was slipping away. He realized that his data might go to waste if he did not take a chance with Kepler and his gift for applying mathematics to astronomy. Perhaps Kepler could do what he could not and make sense of his observations of the orbit of Mars. Brahe's goal was to find a way to make Mars's motion fit with the predictions of his Tychonic system.

TYCHO'S LEGACY

One of Brahe's greatest fears was that his life would be meaningless. Fearing that he did not have much longer to live and wanting to prove his Tychonic system, he finally made a monumental decision. He decided to give Kepler the task of putting together a new table of astronomical data that would be based on his superb observations.

THE ELLIPTICAL ORBIT OF HALLEY'S COMET

Kepler's laws described the details of planetary orbits, but they had nothing to say about what caused planets to move in elliptical paths. In 1687, Isaac Newton (1642–1727) provided the explanation in his famous book *Philosophiae Naturalis Principia Mathematica* (*Mathematical Principles of Natural Philosophy*). Any body orbiting the sun did so because of gravity, and the mathematical form of the law of gravity caused the path to be an ellipse.

Newton's laws permitted all kinds of elliptical orbits—not only the nearly circular orbits of the planet but also long ellipses with their two foci far apart. Astronomer Edmond Halley (1656–1742) realized people had already observed bodies that followed such elongated orbits: comets. He reviewed the history of comets and concluded that the great comets of 1531, 1607, and 1682 were actually the same body. In 1705, he predicted the return of that comet in 1758 and approximately every seventy-six years after that. He was no longer living in 1758, but his prediction came true. Ever since then, that body has been known as Halley's Comet.

Astronomers and historians have examined ancient writings to calculate and identify past appearances of Halley's Comet. In 1981, astronomers Donald Yeomans and Tao Kiang calculated that the comet must have come exceptionally close to Earth in 837 CE. And indeed, Chinese writings from that period have many detailed descriptions of a spectacular "broom star." The oldest record of an approach of Halley's Comet, according to Yeomans and Kiang, was in 240 BCE, again in the Chinese literature. They also found Babylonian writings describing its appearance in 164 BCE and 87 BCE.

Halley's Comet's most recent approach was in 1986, and it will return in 2061. Mark your calendars!

Other astronomical tables had been written in the past, but the *Rudolphine Tables*, which Brahe named after the Roman emperor Rudolf II, would be the most accurate ones the world had ever known. When Kepler finished the task, the *Rudolphine Tables* would be useful for calculating the positions of the planets one thousand years into the past and one thousand years into the future.

Brahe's decision to have Kepler work on the *Rudolphine Tables* turned out to be one of the most momentous in the history of science. To Brahe, it was a way to preserve his legacy. But to Kepler, it was everything he had hoped for when he began his work in Prague but had not received. At last he had access to all of Brahe's data, which he hoped would allow him to discover God's mathematical laws of planetary motion.

NAMED AFTER ROMAN EMPEROR RUDOLF II, JOHANNES KEPLER'S *RUDOLPHINE TABLES* (1627) WAS THE MOST RELIABLE BOOK BY WHICH THE POSITIONS OF THE PLANETS AND STARS COULD BE STUDIED. SHOWN HERE IS THE FRONTISPIECE ILLUSTRATION OF THAT BOOK, WHICH DEPICTS A TEMPLE BUILT ON THE FOUNDATIONS OF THE WORKS OF GREAT ASTRONOMERS OF HISTORY UP TO KEPLER'S TIME. KEPLER HIMSELF IS PICTURED AT THE BOTTOM LEFT.

Only a few weeks after Kepler began his work on the *Rudolphine Tables*, Brahe died. Soon after Brahe's death, Emperor Rudolph II named Kepler to succeed Brahe as the imperial mathematician. Kepler was put in charge of Brahe's instruments, his writings, and his full set of observations. He used the data to finish the *Rudolphine Tables* (in 1627), but not before he completed his work on Mars's orbit.

ELLIPSES REPLACE EPICYCLES

By 1604, Kepler had been studying Brahe's data for three years, but Mars's orbit remained a riddle. He knew that Brahe's measurements were accurate because he had watched him and his assistants at the Prague Observatory checking and double-checking their measurements. However, when he plotted out all the observations, he noticed the data did not fit its orbit into a circular path, even with epicycles. No amount of adjusting made his figures work.

He had, however, made an interesting discovery about how the speed of Mars in its orbit changed. He began with the idea that the planets move under the influence of a force from the sun—what we now know as gravity. Next, he creatively used the observations of Mars to study Earth's orbit. He found that Earth, like the other planets, sped up as it neared the sun and slowed down as it got farther away. He even found a mathematical relationship between the speed of Mars or Earth and its distance from the sun. No matter where the planet was in its orbit, the line between it and the sun swept out the same amount of area in the same amount of time.

It was at that point that Kepler finally began to question the validity of circular orbits with epicycles. He began examining the possibility of oval orbits instead. The particular form of oval called an ellipse worked very well. To draw an ellipse, you take two points, each called a focus (plural: foci) and draw an oval such that the sum of the distances between any point on the oval and the two foci adds up to the same amount no matter which point you choose. If the foci are brought together, the ellipse becomes a circle. By 1605, Kepler was sure he

THIS PAGE FROM BOOK FOUR OF THE SEVEN VOLUME *EPITOME ASTRONOMIAE COPERNICANAE* (*EPITOME OF COPERNICAN ASTRONOMY*, 1621) APPLIES KEPLER'S THIRD LAW TO THE ORBITS OF THE FOUR SATELLITES OF JUPITER THAT HAD BEEN DISCOVERED BY GALILEO.

had the answer. The orbits of Mars and Earth were ellipses with the sun at one focus.

The next step was applying what he discovered to other planets. He realized that their orbits were also ellipses with the sun at one focus and that the lines between them and the sun also swept out equal areas in equal time. Those were his first and second laws of planetary motion. He published them in 1609 in a book called *Astronomia Nova* (*New Astronomy*).

After ten more years of hard work with Brahe's data and his own, Kepler discovered the last of his three laws. It is a mathematical relationship between the size of a planet's orbit and the time it takes to go once around the sun. He published this in 1619 in his book *Harmony of the World*.

Kepler's most influential work was a seven-volume textbook, *Epitome Astronomiae Copernicanae* (*Epitome of Copernican Astronomy*), which was published in 1621. It contained all three of the laws that Kepler developed as a mathematical model for the motion of the planets.

Brahe was correct that Kepler was the right person to carry on his legacy. But the result of Kepler's work was not the preservation of the Tychonic system as he had hoped. Rather it led to the replacement of the geocentric Tychonic system with a heliocentric one governed by Kepler's laws of planetary motion.

CHAPTER FIVE

THE MATHEMATICS OF KEPLER'S LAWS

After Kepler discovered his laws, it became easier for people to accept Copernicus's idea that the sun, not Earth, was at the center of everything. Today, we know that is not true, either. The sun is indeed the center of our solar system, but it is only one of many stars in the Milky Way Galaxy. And the Milky Way is only one of many galaxies in the universe.

But the mathematical forms of Kepler's laws are correct not only for our solar system but also for any system of smaller bodies orbiting a much larger one under the influence of gravity. That includes the moons of Jupiter, which Kepler himself analyzed, and the *Kepler* spacecraft's newly discovered planets around other stars. Let's take a closer look at each of those laws.

KEPLER'S FIRST LAW: THE SHAPE OF PLANETARY ORBITS

As noted in the last section, Kepler improved Copernicus's heliocentric system by eliminating the need for epicycles to match the observed position of the planets in the sky. To do so, he had to give up the idea of planetary motion in perfect circles. He replaced the circles with shapes that are mathematically similar: ellipses.

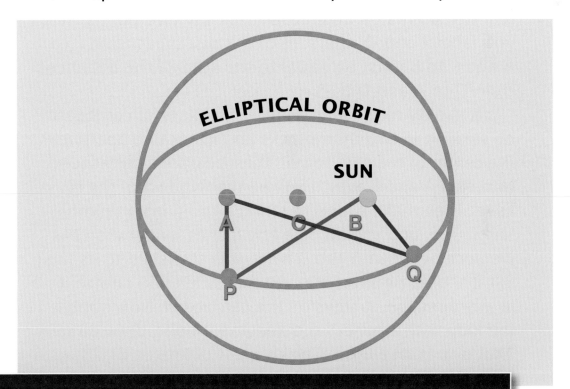

KEPLER'S FIRST LAW OF PLANETARY MOTION STATES THAT THE SHAPE OF A PLANET'S ORBIT IS AN ELLIPSE WITH THE SUN AT ONE FOCUS, WHICH MEANS THAT THE DISTANCE BETWEEN THE PLANET AND THE SUN CHANGES AS THE PLANET FOLLOWS ITS PATH. FOR EVERY POINT ON AN ELLIPSE, ADDING THE DISTANCES BETWEEN THAT POINT AND THE TWO FOCI PRODUCES THE SAME SUM. WHEN THE TWO FOCI OF AN ELLIPSE ARE CLOSE TOGETHER, THE ORBIT IS NEARLY CIRCULAR. WHEN THEY OVERLAP, THE ORBIT IS A PERFECT CIRCLE.

A circle can be described as the set of points on a flat surface that are all the same distance from another point called the center. If you draw a diagram of a circle, the center of the circle can be marked C. To get an ellipse from that circle, replace the center point with two points on the circle that are directly opposite each other and that you can label A and B. Now stretch the circle so that it becomes an oval, with its longest distance along the line connecting A and B.

Not just any oval will do as an ellipse. If you choose any two points on an ellipse—let's say two points that you label P and Q, the sum of the distances from P to A and P to B must be equal to the sum of the distances from Q to A and Q to B.

It is easy to draw an ellipse on a piece of cardboard by sticking in two thumbtacks an inch or two apart near the center of the cardboard. Their positions correspond to points A and B, which will be the two foci of the ellipse. Then make a loop of string around both thumbtacks. The loop should be a few inches longer than the distance between A and B when it is stretched to its limit. But it should be short enough that when you stretch it in any direction, it stays on the cardboard. Now stretch the loop with a pencil, and keeping it tight, draw an oval. That oval is an ellipse. The shortest diameter, or distance from end to end, across the ellipse is called the minor axis. The longest diameter is called the major axis.

If the pencil point represents a planet, then one of the thumbtacks is the sun. The farther apart the two foci are compared to the length of the string, the more elongated is the ellipse. If the two thumbtacks are so close together that they overlap, the ellipse becomes a circle. A circle is an ellipse with its major and minor axes equal to each other.

In the solar system, the orbits of the planets have different elongations. The orbit of Venus is closest to a circle, followed by the orbits of Neptune and Earth. Mars's

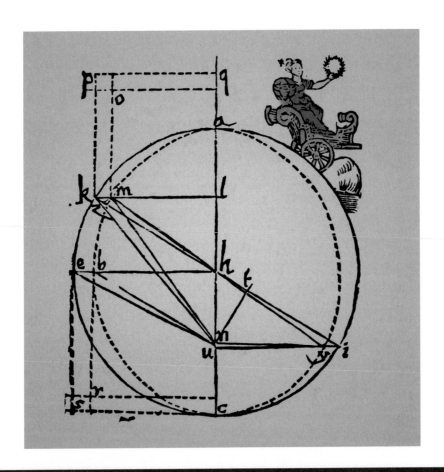

THIS DIAGRAM SHOWS KEPLER'S ANALYSIS OF THE ORBIT OF MARS, WHICH APPEARS AS THE DASHED ELLIPSE INSIDE THE SOLID CIRCLE. THE POINTS LABELED L AND N ARE THE FOCI, WHILE H IS THE CENTER OF THE CIRCLE AND THE ELLIPSE. THE SUN IS AT POINT N. POINTS A AND C ARE MARS'S APHELION AND PERIHELION (ITS FARTHEST DISTANCE FROM AND CLOSEST APPROACH TO THE SUN), RESPECTIVELY.

orbit is the most elongated, with Mercury's coming next. Many other objects orbiting the sun have more elongated orbits than Mars. For instance, when the dwarf planet Pluto was considered a major planet, it held the title of the most elongated planetary orbit.

If the orbit of Mars had been as close to circular as Venus's, Kepler would have had a harder time discovering his first law. The measurements he used were not as precise as the ones that could be made later with telescopes. So he might have been able to match a nearly circular orbit with epicycles instead of needing an ellipse to correctly describe Mars's orbit.

WHEN IS EARTH CLOSEST TO THE SUN?

The point at which a solar system body is closest to the sun in its orbit is called the perihelion. Its farthest point is the aphelion. Earth currently reaches perihelion in early January, and it is the farthest from the sun in July. Because of the gravitational influence of other planets, the perihelion moves slowly through the year. In about fifty-six thousand years, the perihelion and aphelion dates will be reversed.

If you live in the Northern Hemisphere, you might be surprised that Earth is closest to the sun in midwinter. Nevertheless, midwinter remains a typically cold and dark season in the Northern Hemisphere because the tilt of Earth's axis away from the sun at this time makes a much bigger difference to the amount of sunlight than does Earth's relative proximity (nearness) to the sun.

Orbits of comets are usually much more elongated than those of the planets. For instance, the most famous comet is named after the great astronomer Edmond Halley. At its greatest distance from the sun (or aphelion), it is farther away than Neptune; at its nearest point (perihelion), it comes almost as close to the sun as Mercury does.

KEPLER'S SECOND LAW: CHANGING SPEEDS, CONSTANT AREAS

As noted in the previous section, Kepler discovered what we now call his second law of planetary motion before the first. Measurements showed him that the speed of Mars was changing as it orbited the sun. It went faster when it was closer to the sun's influence and slower when farther away. He looked for a mathematical relationship between distance and speed and quickly found what can be called the law of equal areas. He later discovered that it applies not to Mars alone but to every planet in the solar system.

Kepler visualized the line between the planet and the sun as the planet followed its elliptical path. Each minute (or any short period of time you want to choose), that line would trace out a segment of the ellipse shaped like a piece of pie. When the planet is

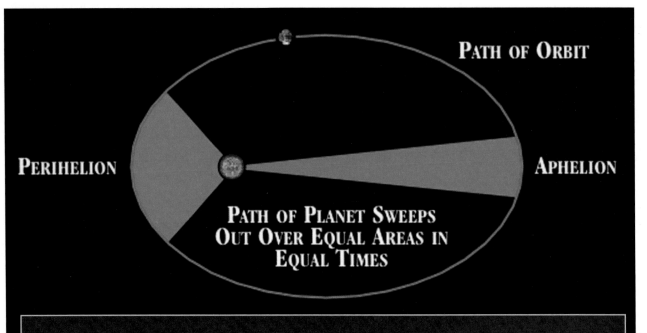

PATH OF ORBIT

PERIHELION

APHELION

PATH OF PLANET SWEEPS
OUT OVER EQUAL AREAS IN
EQUAL TIMES

KEPLER'S SECOND LAW, KNOWN AS THE LAW OF EQUAL AREAS, IS ILLUSTRATED HERE. AS THE DISTANCES OF PLANETS FROM THE SUN CHANGE AS THEY GO AROUND THEIR ELLIPTICAL PATHS, SO DO THEIR SPEEDS. THEY GO FASTER WHEN CLOSER TO THE SUN AND SLOWER WHEN FARTHER AWAY. WHAT DOES REMAIN CONSTANT IS THE RATE AT WHICH THE LINE BETWEEN THE SUN AND PLANET SWEEPS OUT AREA. THE GREEN SECTORS REPRESENT EQUAL PERIODS OF TIME NEAR THE APHELION AND PERIHELION. BECAUSE THE PLANET MOVES FASTEST NEAR ITS PERIHELION, THE ANGLE OF THAT SECTOR IS LARGER THAN THE ANGLE AT ITS APHELION. THE AREAS, HOWEVER, ARE THE SAME.

closer to the sun, it moves faster, so the angle of the segment is larger. When the planet is farther away, it moves more slowly, so the angle of the segment is smaller. The combination of the smaller length and the larger angle turns out to be perfectly matched so that the areas of the segments are exactly the same. It is as if the planet is eating an elliptical pie at a precise and unchanging rate even though the bites have different shapes.

THE LENGTH OF EARTH'S SEASONS AND THE LAW OF EQUAL AREAS

Since Earth is closest to the sun in the northern winter, the law of equal areas tells you that it is moving fastest at that time. That means the number of days from the beginning of the northern fall (approximately September 22) to the beginning of northern spring (approximately March 20) should be just slightly less than the number of days from spring to fall. Using your calendar, you can discover this is true (181 days versus 184).

KEPLER'S THIRD LAW: HOW PLANETARY ORBITS RELATE TO EACH OTHER

Kepler also realized that the farther a planet is from the sun, the longer it takes to complete one orbit. Mercury and Venus are closer than Earth, so they complete their orbits in less than a year. Mars, Jupiter, and Saturn are farther out, and their orbital periods are longer. These were the only planets that Kepler knew about.

He looked for a mathematical formula that would relate the orbital period of a planet to its distance from the sun. He could easily see that it was not as simple as a direct proportion, which would state that twice the distance corresponds to twice the orbital period. But to a mathematical mind like Kepler's, it was not difficult to discover a different direct proportion that fit the measurements.

His third law states that the square of a planet's orbital period (the period multiplied by itself) is directly proportional to the cube of the planet's average distance

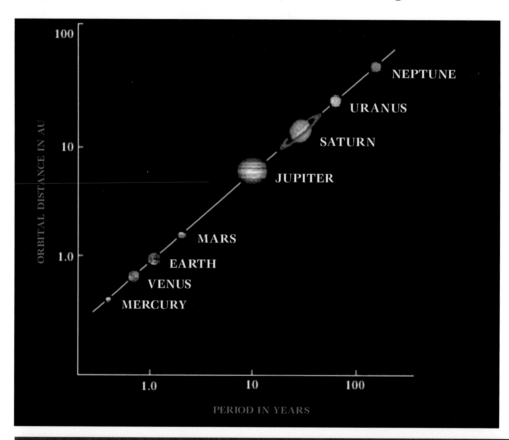

THIS GRAPH ILLUSTRATES KEPLER'S THIRD LAW FOR THE PLANETS OF THE SOLAR SYSTEM. IT USES A SPECIAL KIND OF SCALE CALLED A LOGARITHMIC SCALE ON BOTH THE HORIZONTAL AND VERTICAL AXIS BECAUSE KEPLER'S THIRD LAW IS A STRAIGHT LINE ON SUCH A GRAPH. ON A LOGARITHMIC SCALE, THE SPACING BETWEEN TICK MARKS REPRESENTS MULTIPLICATION BY TEN. INSTEAD OF BEING NUMBERED 1, 2, 3, THE TICK MARKS ARE NUMBERED 1, 10, 100, AND SO FORTH. THE HORIZONTAL AXIS ON THIS GRAPH IS THE TIME IN YEARS THAT IT TAKES EACH PLANET TO COMPLETE ITS ORBIT. THE VERTICAL AXIS IS THE DISTANCE BETWEEN THE PLANET AND THE SUN IN ASTRONOMICAL UNITS, WHERE ONE AU IS THE DISTANCE FROM EARTH TO THE SUN.

from the sun (the distance multiplied by itself, then multiplied by itself again). This is sometimes called the harmonic law. That term fits with a mathematical definition but also with Kepler's religious beliefs that the planets moved in a harmony established by God.

His third law can be written as a mathematical equation:

$$P^2 = d^3$$

Here, P represents a planet's orbital period, the time in Earth years that it takes for the planet to go once around the sun. The d represents the planet's average distance from the sun measured in astronomical units, or AU. One AU is the average distance between Earth and the sun.

In this equation, the orbital period (P) is squared. The square of a number is that number multiplied by itself. In other words: P times P. In the equation, the distance (d) is cubed. This means d times d times d (d multiplied by itself three times).

For Earth, P=1 year and d=1 AU, so the equation states the obvious: 1 squared is equal to 1 cubed. For Mars, d=1.52 AU and P=1.88 years, rounded off to the second decimal place. That gives P^2=3.51 and d^3=3.53. The small difference between those numbers comes from the rounding. When we use the best measurements of modern astronomy for every planet in the solar system, P^2 and d^3 are always equal to each other.

CHAPTER SIX

KEPLER'S OTHER ACCOMPLISHMENTS AND MODERN SCIENCE

*T*oday, Johannes Kepler is best known for his three laws of planetary motion, but he had other accomplishments as well. His influence was great in his own time, and it continues even today.

Besides being a pioneering astronomer, Kepler also deserves credit for several "firsts" in the field of optics, which is the science and technology of light. In 1604, he published the book *Astronomiae Pars Optica* (*The Optical Part of Astronomy*). In it, he described many of his optical discoveries.

Kepler was the first person to investigate the formation of images with a device called a pinhole camera. He was also the first person to correctly explain how an image is formed in the human eye. He discovered that the objects we see are projected upside down and backward on the retina, the back part of the eye.

He also was the first to figure out how to use differently shaped eyeglasses to correct nearsightedness (difficulty seeing objects that are far away) and farsightedness (difficulty seeing objects that are close up). This topic was an especially personal one for Kepler, having worn spectacles himself.

He later applied the ideas from *Astronomiae Pars Optica* to the telescope. He described this work in his book *Dioptrice* (*Dioptrics*; 1611). Kepler did not invent the telescope, nor was he the first to use it in astronomy. But he was the first to explain the principles of how it works. Inside a telescope are many lenses and mirrors that gather light and allow people to observe objects that are very far away. Kepler's work began the new field of science called dioptrics, the science of refraction by lenses (refraction is the turning or bending of light). The idea of dioptrics was later used by other scientists to better understand the function of the eye and to make improvements on the telescope.

FROM KEPLER TO NEWTON

In pondering why the planets changed speed as they orbited the sun, Kepler settled on an explanation that was more religious than scientific or mathematical. He wrote that the sun, which he saw as the representation of God, exerts some kind of force on the planets that diminishes as the planets get farther away from the sun (just as proximity to God would presumably draw the believer closer to Him, whereas greater distance would reduce or dilute God's powerful influence). Still, this idea laid the foundation for Sir Isaac Newton's discovery of the principles of gravity.

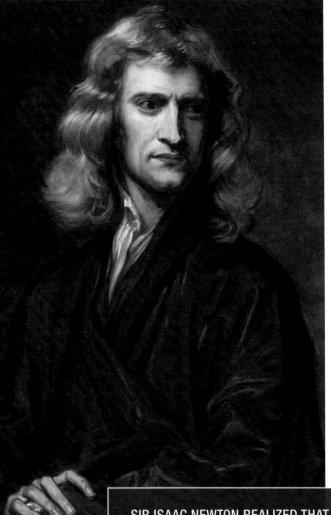

Although Kepler's laws explained how the planets move around the sun, they did not include a mathematical description of the sun's influence on the planets. It took Isaac Newton to recognize that planetary motion was governed by gravity, the same force that causes objects to fall on Earth. Newton realized that all objects attract each other by gravitation. He showed that the bigger the objects, the stronger they pull on each other. He also realized

SIR ISAAC NEWTON REALIZED THAT THE ATTRACTIVE FORCE OF GRAVITY BETWEEN TWO BODIES WAS INVERSELY PROPORTIONAL TO THE SQUARE OF THE DISTANCE BETWEEN THEM. IF THEY WERE TWICE AS FAR APART, THE FORCE WAS ONE-FOURTH (ONE PART IN 2X2) AS STRONG. WHEN HE APPLIED THAT RELATIONSHIP TO THE SOLAR SYSTEM, HE FOUND THAT THE PLANETS HAD ELLIPTICAL ORBITS AND FOLLOWED KEPLER'S OTHER TWO LAWS.

DO KEPLER'S LAWS WORK IN OTHER SOLAR SYSTEMS?

In the *Principia*, Isaac Newton explained that his laws of motion and gravity led exactly to Kepler's laws. In fact, Newton showed that Kepler's laws would be valid for any system of bodies orbiting a large central body, such as the moons orbiting Jupiter. The smaller bodies would follow elliptical orbits. The line from the central body to any orbiting body would obey the law of equal areas.

The only difference in Kepler's laws when considering another solar system is in the constant of proportionality between P^2 and d^3 in the third law. That constant depends on the mass of the central body. Today, astronomers are beginning to discover hundreds of planets orbiting other stars. By measuring a planet's rotational period and the distance between it and the star, they can determine the proportionality constant in Kepler's Third Law for that star. Knowing that constant tells them how heavy the star is.

Incidentally, many of those alien planets have been detected by a planet-hunting space observatory called *Kepler*, which was launched in 2009.

that the farther apart the objects are, the weaker is the force between them. He wrote that the strength of the force follows an inverse square law. This means that if the objects are twice as far apart, their attraction is diminished to one-fourth ($4 = 2 \times 2$). If they are three times as far apart, the force is only one-ninth ($9 = 3 \times 3$) as strong, and so on.

Newton computed the motion of planets in a solar system governed by gravity that followed the mathematical form of his law of universal gravitation, and the results validated Kepler's three laws. As noted in the earlier discussion of Halley's Comet, this was one of many important results in Newton's classic book from 1687, *Philosophiae Naturalis Principia Mathematica* (*Mathematical Principles of Natural Philosophy*), often called simply the *Principia*.

KEPLER'S CONTRIBUTIONS TO MATHEMATICS

Kepler also made many important discoveries in the field of mathematics. One of these was a method for finding the volumes of solids. Volume is the amount of space that something takes up. Kepler's inspiration to study this subject came from an odd source.

At his wedding, he noticed many differently shaped wine barrels. He learned that the volumes of the barrels were estimated by measuring only their diagonal lengths. The shapes of the barrels were disregarded. Kepler wondered how that could work. His pondering led him to write *Stereometria Doliorum Vinariorum* (*The Stereometry of Wine Barrels*). Though this book was not hugely popular at the time, it became a very important step in the development of integral calculus, a type of math that is used for figuring out things such as volume and area.

Kepler was a brilliant mathematician. Tycho Brahe recognized this, and that is why he put him in charge of his valuable observations. Using his mathematical talents, Kepler was able to unlock the secrets that were hidden in Brahe's data and produce his world-changing laws of planetary motion, as well as many other mathematical laws.

KEPLER AND THE SCIENCE OF ASTRONOMY

In Kepler's time, astronomy and astrology were considered two aspects of the same science. As noted earlier, he was probably one of the first to draw a distinction between them. Although he made astrological predictions, he understood that science requires the testing of ideas against actual observations.

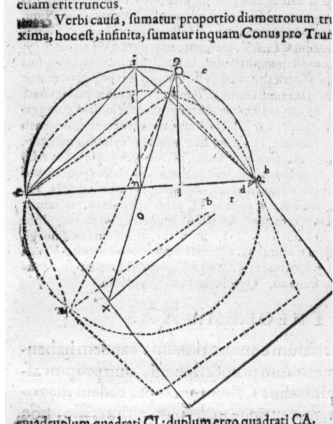

THIS DIAGRAM IS FROM KEPLER'S BOOK *STEREOMETRIA DOLIORUM VINARIORUM* (1615), WHICH DISCUSSED HOW TO COMPUTE THE VOLUME OF VARIOUS SHAPES AND LED TO THE DEVELOPMENT OF THE BRANCH OF MATHEMATICS KNOWN AS INTEGRAL CALCULUS.

That is why the opportunity to work with Brahe was so important to him. Brahe's observatory had the finest instruments of its time, and Brahe's observations filled many pages of record books. When Kepler succeeded Brahe, he continued adding to that great storehouse of data. By studying and adding to the observations for years, Kepler was able to develop mathematical descriptions of planetary motion, which ultimately became his three laws of planetary motion.

Others may have been reluctant to accept those laws, but, like the best scientists of today and throughout history, Kepler had the observational data to back them up. His laws of planetary motion marked the beginning of a revolutionary way of viewing the universe. By replacing

TYCHO BRAHE HIRED KEPLER IN THE HOPE THAT KEPLER'S MATHEMATICAL SKILLS WOULD SUPPORT THE TYCHONIC MODEL OF THE UNIVERSE. INSTEAD, KEPLER'S LAWS SHOWED THAT A MODIFIED COPERNICAN MODEL GAVE A BETTER DESCRIPTION OF THE MOTION OF THE BODIES OF THE SOLAR SYSTEM. BUT KEPLER ALSO CEMENTED THE REPUTATION OF BRAHE'S OBSERVATORY AND THE DATA IT GATHERED AS AMONG THE MOST IMPORTANT IN THE HISTORY OF ASTRONOMY.

epicycles with ellipses, Kepler transformed Copernicus's flawed conception of the heliocentric universe into a form that was hard to deny, even though it conflicted with the teachings of his church.

Unlike many astronomers who came before him, Kepler was true to his data. When the observations that Brahe had given him did not match old theories that required planets to move in complicated combinations of perfect circles, he did not try to force the observations into even more complicated versions of those theories. He did not try to shape the data to fit his theories. Rather, he shaped his theories according to the available data. He sought to develop mathematical explanations that would fit naturally with the data that he and Brahe had collected. This was a revolutionary way of approaching scientific research, and it changed the way that scientists work to this day. Remarkably, Kepler pursued his revolutionary theories even while remaining loyal to his own religious faith, a faith that often stood in stark contradiction to the discoveries of science. Until the day he died in 1630, he continued to believe that his mathematical formulas provided a way to understand the mind of God.

Whether or not they share his faith or are even religious, all modern astronomers acknowledge their debt to Johannes Kepler. His pioneering spirit, diligent observation, and creative thinking have earned him the designation as the father of modern astronomy.

1517 Martin Luther begins the Protestant Reformation by posting a list of complaints against the Catholic Church.

1571 Johannes Kepler is born on December 27.

1577 Kepler sees his first comet.

1589 Attends the University of Tübingen.

1594 Goes to Graz to teach mathematics.

1596 Publishes *Mysterium cosmographicum* (*Cosmographic Mystery*).

1600 Goes to Prague to work with Tycho Brahe.

1601 Brahe dies.

Kepler writes *De Fundamentis Astrologiae Certioribus* (*Concerning the More Certain Fundamentals of Astrology*).

1604 Publishes *Astronomiae Pars Optica* (*The Optical Part of Astronomy*).

1609 Publishes *Astronomia Nova* (*New Astronomy*).

1611 Publishes *Dioptrice* (*Dioptrics*).

1615 Publishes *Stereometria Doliorum Vinariorum* (*The Stereometry of Wine Barrels*).

1618 The Thirty Years' War begins.

1619 Kepler publishes *Harmonice Mundi* (*Harmony of the World*).

1621 Publishes *Epitome Astronomiae Copernicanae* (*Epitome of Copernican Astronomy*).

1627 Publishes the *Rudolphine Tables*.

1630 Kepler dies on November 15.

1651 Astronomer Giovanni Battista Riccioli (1598–1671) publishes the *New Almagest*, which includes a map of the moon. Riccioli names one of the largest craters after Kepler.

1758 Halley's Comet returns, demonstrating that its elliptical orbit obeys Kepler's laws.

1929 Max Wolf discovers an asteroid that is given the official name 1134 Kepler.

1966 A college that has become Johannes Kepler University is founded in Linz, Austria.

1973 A 145-mile (233-km) crater on Mars is named in honor of Kepler.

2009 NASA launches the *Kepler* planet-hunting spacecraft to search for planets orbiting other stars.

2012 *Kepler* spacecraft discovers its one hundredth confirmed planet, ends its primary mission, and begins its extended mission.

2013 Count of planetary candidates detected by *Kepler* spacecraft passes 2,700.

2016 Scheduled end of *Kepler* spacecraft's extended mission.

GLOSSARY

APHELION The point in the orbit of a planet that is farthest from the sun.

ARMILLARY SPHERE A historical astronomical instrument composed of rings representing the important circles of the celestial sphere.

ASTROLOGY The study of the movement of heavenly bodies with the belief that they influence people's lives.

ASTRONOMY The scientific study of space and objects in space.

AXIS A straight line passing through the center of a body around which the body rotates.

COMET A body in the solar system made of ice, dust, and gas that follows a very elongated orbit around the sun.

CUBE The product of one number when multiplied by itself three times.

DEFERENT A circle centered on the point halfway between Earth and the equant, used in Ptolemy's geocentric description of the universe as a planet's main motion.

ECLIPSE The phenomenon that occurs when one heavenly body passes in front of another so that the light of one heavenly body is blocked.

EPICYCLE A circle around a point on the deferent used to explain the paths of the sun, moon, and planets in Ptolemy's geocentric description of the universe.

EQUANT A point used in Ptolemy's geocentric description of the universe to explain the sun's changing speed around Earth at different times of the year. Ptolemy stated that the sun changed the angle it made with the line between the equant and Earth at a constant rate.

FOCUS One of two fixed points around which an ellipse is formed.

GALAXY A system of many billions of stars held together by gravity.

GEOCENTRIC A description of the universe that places Earth at its center.

GRAVITY A force of attraction that exists between any two objects that have mass.

HELIOCENTRIC A description of the universe that places the sun at its center.

OBSERVATORY A building designed to house astronomical instruments.

ORBIT The path an object takes as it revolves around another object.

PERIHELION The point in the orbit of a planet at which it is closest to the sun.

PLATONIC SOLID One of the five possible geometric solid figures that has all faces identical, with all sides the same length and all angles the same.

PROPORTIONAL Having the same ratio.

QUADRANT An astronomical instrument used for measuring the angle of an object above the horizon.

REFORMER A person who is trying to change a system or belief for the better.

SEXTANT An astronomical instrument used for measuring angular distances between objects in the sky.

SQUARE The product of one number when multiplied by itself.

VOLUME The amount of space occupied by an object.

FOR MORE INFORMATION

American Astronomical Society (AAS)

2000 Florida Avenue NW, Suite 400

Washington, DC 20009

(202) 328-2010

Web site: http://www.aas.org

The mission of the AAS is to enhance and share humanity's scientific understanding of the universe. It sponsors meetings and publishes journals for scientists and publishes information for the public, educators, and people interested in careers in astronomy.

American Institute of Physics (AIP)

One Physics Ellipse

College Park, MD 20740-3843

(301) 209-3100

Web site: http://www.aip.org

The AIP is the umbrella organization for many different professional societies of physical scientists. It publishes journals for scientists and magazines for educators, the public, and students interested in careers in physics. Its Center for the History of Physics contains a library and archive of historical books and photographs.

Kepler Museum

Prague, Karlova 4

Czech Republic

Phone: +420 608 971 236

Web site: http://www.keplerovomuzeum.cz

This museum was founded in the International Year of Astronomy, 2009, with the professional and organizational support of the Czech Astronomic Society. The three circles in the logo of the Kepler Museum represent Mars, Earth, and the sun. These are the bodies whose mutual positions were studied by Kepler in Prague.

Planetary Society

85 South Grand Avenue

Pasadena, CA 91105

(626) 793-5100

Web site: http://www.planetary.org

The Planetary Society's executive director, Bill Nye ("The Science Guy"), describes society this way: "Who are we? We are YOU! We are wowed and awed by the discovery of new things, the mysteries of science, the innovations of technology, the bravery of astronauts, and by the stunning images sent back to us from other worlds. We know that space exploration is vital to humankind...and it is just plain fun!"

Royal Astronomical Society of Canada (RASC)

203-4920 Dundas Street West

Toronto, ON M9A 1B7

Canada

(888) 924-7272 (in Canada)

(416) 924-7973 (outside Canada)

Web site: http://www.rasc.ca

The RASC aims to inspire curiosity in all Canadians about the universe, share scientific knowledge, and foster understanding of astronomy through activities, including education, research, and community outreach activities. Its publications and extensive Web site have materials for scientists, researchers, teachers, and students.

WEB SITES

Due to the changing nature of Internet links, Rosen Publishing has developed an online list of Web sites related to the subject of this book. This site is updated regularly. Please use this link to access the list:

http://www.rosenlinks.com/RDSP/kepler

FOR FURTHER READING

Anderson, Michael. *Pioneers in Astronomy and Space Exploration.* New York, NY: Brittanica Educational Publishing, 2013.

Bortz, Fred. *Seven Wonders of Exploration Technology.* Minneapolis, MN: Twenty-First Century Books, 2010.

Bortz, Fred. *Seven Wonders of Space Technology.* Minneapolis, MN: Twenty-First Century Books, 2011.

Curley, Robert. *Scientists and Inventors of the Renaissance.* New York, NY: Brittanica Educational Publishing, 2013.

Miller, Ron. *Recentering the Universe: The Radical Theories of Copernicus, Kepler, and Galileo.* Minneapolis, MN: Twenty-First Century Books, 2014.

Miller, Ron. *Seven Wonders of Asteroids, Comets, and Meteors.* Minneapolis, MN: Twenty-First Century Books, 2011.

Robinson, Andrew, ed. *The Scientists: An Epic of Discovery.* New York, NY: Thames and Hudson, 2012.

Timmons, Todd. *Makers of Western Science: The Works and Words of 24 Visionaries from Copernicus to Watson and Crick.* Jefferson, NC: McFarland & Co., 2012.

Wilkins, Jamie, and Robert Dunn. *300 Astronomical Objects: A Visual Reference to the Universe.* Richmond Hill, ON, Canada: Firefly Books, 2011.

BBC. "Edmond Halley." Retrieved February 2013 (http://www.bbc.co.uk/history/historic_figures/halley_edmond.shtml).

Boerst, William J. *Johannes Kepler: Discovering the Laws of Celestial Motion.* Greensboro, NC: Morgan Reynolds Publishing, 2003.

Boss, Alan. *The Crowded Universe: The Search for Living Planets.* New York, NY: Basic Books, 2009.

Caspar, Max. *Kepler* (trans. and ed., C. Doris Hellman). New York, NY: Dover, 1993.

Cropper, William H. *Great Physicists: The Life and Times of Leading Physicists from Galileo to Hawking.* New York, NY: Oxford University Press, 2001.

Ferguson, Kitty. *Tycho & Kepler: The Unlikely Partnership That Forever Changed Our Understanding of the Heavens.* New York, NY: Walker & Company, 2002.

Field, J. V. "Johannes Kepler." School of Mathematical and Computational Sciences, University of St. Andrews. Retrieved February 2013 (http://turnbull.mcs.st-and.ac.uk/history/Biographies/Kepler.html).

Fowler, Michael. "Johannes Kepler." University of Virginia, 1995. Retrieved February 2013 (http://galileo.phys.virginia.edu/classes/109N/1995/lectures/kepler.html).

Frankenberry, Nancy, ed. *The Faith of Scientists: In Their Own Words.* Princeton, NJ: Princeton University Press, 2008.

Moore, Patrick. *Men of the Stars.* New York, NY: Gallery Books, 1986.

NASA. "Kepler: A Search for Habitable Planets." Retrieved February 2013 (http://www.nasa.gov/mission _pages/kepler/main/index.html).

Nicolson, Iain. *Unfolding Our Universe.* Cambridge, England: Cambridge University Press, 1999.

Ridpath, Ian. *A Comet Called Halley.* Cambridge, England: Cambridge University Press, 1985.

Ridpath, Ian, ed. *Oxford Dictionary of Astronomy.* 2nd ed. New York, NY: Oxford University Press, 2007.

Sullivan, Navin. *Pioneer Astronomers.* New York, NY: The Murray Printing Company, 1964.

INDEX

A

Almagest, 12, 16
anti-Semitism, 25
aphelion, 52, 53
Aristarchus, 32
Aristotle, 14, 15, 16, 26, 32
astrology, 30, 31, 63
Astronomia Nova, 47
Astronomiae Pars Optica, 58, 59

B

Brahe, Tycho, 24, 25, 26, 31, 37, 38–47, 62–63, 64, 65

C

calendars, 28–30, 55
comets, 10, 43, 53, 62
Copernicus, Nicolaus, 11, 17, 19, 25, 31, 32, 33, 34, 37, 38, 40, 48, 49, 65
Counter-Reformation, 23–24

D

De Fundamentis Astrologiae Certiorbus, 30
De Revolutionibus, 11, 17, 31
Dioptrice, 59

E

Epitome Astronomiae Copernicanae, 47
equal areas, law of, 53–54
Eudoxus, 14, 15, 16
eyeglasses, shaping of, 59

F

Ferdinand II, 23

G

galaxies, 48
Galileo, 34, 37
geocentric view of universe, 12–16, 32
gravity, 6, 43, 45, 48, 52, 60, 61, 62

H

Halley, Edmond, 43, 53
Halley's Comet, 43, 53, 62
harmonic law, 57
Harmony of the World, 28, 47
heliocentric view of universe, 11, 19, 31, 32–34, 37, 38, 40, 47, 49, 65
Hirschfield, Alan W., 34
Hitler, Adolf, 25, 26

J

Jupiter, 4, 15, 19, 36, 48, 55, 61

K

Kepler, Johannes,
   early career, 18–19, 23–37
   early life, 7–17
   laws of planetary motion,
      8, 11, 19, 23, 31, 47,
      48–57, 63, 64
   other accomplishments,
      58–65
   overview, 4–6
   religious beliefs, 12, 24,
      26–27, 44, 57, 59–
      60, 65
   work with Brahe, 38–47
Kepler, Heinrich, 7, 8
Kepler, Katharina, 7, 8, 10, 28
Kepler spacecraft, 48, 61
Kiang, Tao, 43

L

Luther, Martin, 22, 23

M

Maestlin, Michael, 12, 17, 18
major axis, 50

Mars, 4, 15, 19, 38, 40, 42, 45,
   46, 47, 51, 52, 53, 55, 57
Mercury, 4, 15, 19, 52, 53, 55
Middle Ages, 11, 32
Milky Way Galaxy, 48
minor axis, 50
Mysterium Cosmographicum,
   34, 37, 40

N

Nazi Party, 25, 26
Neptune, 51, 53
Newton, Isaac, 43, 60–62

O

observatories, 40, 45, 64

P

Parallax, 34
Peace of Augsburg, 22–23
perihelion, 52, 53
*Philosphiae Naturalis Principia
   Mathematica*, 43, 61, 62
pinhole cameras, 58
planetary motion, laws of, 8,
   11, 19, 23, 31, 47, 48–57
Plato, 14, 15, 26
Platonic solids, 36
Prague Observatory, 45

Protestant Reformation, 22
Ptolemy, Claudius, 12, 14, 16, 17, 26, 37, 38, 40

R

Renaissance, 11
religion vs. science, 7, 11, 20–31, 32–34
Roman Catholic Church, 7, 20, 22–26, 31, 32
Rudolf II, 44, 45
Rudolphine Tables, 44, 45

S

Saturn, 4, 15, 19, 36, 55
seasons, changing of, 55
Stereometria Doliorum Vinariorum, 62

T

telescopes, 52, 59
Thirty Years' War, 23, 28
Tychonic system, 38, 40, 42, 47

V

vault of heaven, 15
Venus, 4, 15, 19, 51, 52, 55

W

witch hunting, 28
World War II, 26

Y

Yeomans, Donald, 43

ABOUT THE AUTHOR

After earning his Ph.D. at Carnegie Mellon University in 1971, physicist Fred Bortz set off on an interesting and varied twenty-five year career in teaching and research. From 1979 to 1994, he was on staff at Carnegie Mellon, where his work evolved from research to outreach.

Bortz turned to full-time writing in 1996. His books, now numbering nearly thirty, have won awards, including the American Institute of Physics Science Writing Award, and recognition on several best books lists.

Known on the Internet as the smiling, bowtie-wearing "Dr. Fred," he welcomes inquisitive visitors to his Web site at www.fredbortz.com.

PHOTO CREDITS